How to Study Effectively

Christopher Parsons

How to Study Effectively

Arrow Books

Arrow Books Limited
3 Fitzroy Square, London W1

An imprint of the Hutchinson Publishing Group

London Melbourne Sydney Auckland
Wellington Johannesburg and agencies
throughout the world

First published 1976
Second impression 1977
© Christopher Parsons 1976

Made and printed in Great Britain by litho
by The Anchor Press Ltd, Tiptree, Essex

ISBN 0 09 912400 9

– J. M. Foster

Contents

Acknowledgements

The author is grateful to the following for permission to
reproduce copyright material:

The Artemis Press Ltd
A. D. Peters & Co
Teach Yourself Books Ltd
UNESCO

He would also like to thank Janelle Cooper and Alf Woods
of Hammersmith and West London College for some helpful
suggestions, Jack Hughes for reading the manuscript, and his
wife, Claire, for typing it.

Introduction

This book is a simple guide to the basic techniques of study. It is for any student beginning a course of study at a school, college, adult education institute, polytechnic or university, but should be particularly useful for people who spend much of their study time working on their own, and people who have not studied for several years and need to learn again how to.

Research has shown that, although ability and effort are very important, knowing how to study usually decides whether you get the full benefit from your course and pass your examinations.

This is a work book. It provides training in all the skills of study including planning, note-making, ways of memorizing facts, writing essays, and passing examinations. Read Chapters 1–4 at the beginning of the course and Chapters 5–7 shortly afterwards. Read the last chapter about two months before examinations. Keep this book for regular reference with your other course books.

If you carry out all the instructions, you will stand a much better chance of getting the most from your study course.

1. Starting to Study

There are many skills to learn if you are to become a successful student. They are:

  (a) planning your time
  (b) using the library
  (c) using books
  (d) taking good notes
  (e) memorizing facts and ideas
  (f) writing essays
  (g) taking an examination.

All these skills are explained in this book.

Before you begin your course, you must first do three things:

  (a) clarify in your own mind why you have become a student (your motives)
  (b) find out all you can about your course (course details)
  (c) buy the basic equipment you need.

Motives

Let us begin with your reasons for becoming a student. One of the reasons why students do not get the most out of their courses is that their desire to do so is not strong enough. If you are going to be successful, your desire to succeed must be very strong indeed. So you should begin by working out in your own mind your own special reasons for studying.

Why did you become a student? Why did you start this particular course? In what way is this course going to help you? Why do you want to pass the examinations?

Before you read further, pause for a minute and think about these questions. Then describe briefly in the space below how you came to start your course. Answer the questions in the paragraph above first.

HOW I CAME TO START THIS COURSE

To further my career
I enjoy teaching
I'm in a rut
To further my knowledge
To improve my "
To help others better.

Here are some of the reasons students give for starting a course.

- (a) It seemed like a good idea.
- (b) The social life is good.
- (c) I liked the subject.
- (d) I wanted to become a . . . .
- (e) I was advised to do so by the careers service.
- (f) I wanted to increase my knowledge.
- (g) My friends were there.
- (h) I wanted a qualification.
- (i) My parents wanted me to do it.
- (j) The sports facilities are good.
- (k) I could not make up my mind about a career.
- (l) I wanted to learn more about . . . .

When you read through this list, you may think some reasons sound better than others. Rearrange the list, putting those you think are good reasons on the left and those you think are bad on the right.

GOOD REASONS   BAD REASONS

If you started your course because 'the social life is good', your interest in the course itself may be small. On the other hand, if you have a strong appetite for knowledge or a particular career in mind, then your interest will be very strong and your chances of success will be much greater.

11

The way to increase your desire to succeed is to think about the benefits which will come from completing the course.

What are these? Write them down here.

Know how to teach
Broader outlook
New Job
More money

Now think again about why you are a student. Write in the space below the *main reasons* why you started the course.

THE MAIN REASONS WHY I STARTED THE COURSE

Know how to teach
Broader outlook.
New job
Further knowledge.
Further career

There will be many times when a subject seems boring or becomes difficult, and you may want to stop studying and perhaps give the course up altogether. When you feel like this, look at this page again.

Course Details

Many students do not know very much about the courses they have started. This ignorance may easily stop you getting all you should out of the course. Get a copy of the syllabus and the regulations. Find out the answers to the following questions NOW, and write in the information here.

1. What is the full title of the course?

   Clinical Teachers Course FCT3

2. Which subjects are compulsory?

   Psychology   Physiology

3. Which subjects are optional?

4. Are you assessed? If so, how? Examination only/Examination and course work/Course work only/Other means

   Yes   All means.

5. Do you have to complete a project? If so, what are the requirements? Does it count towards the assessment? What is the deadline for its submission?

   4 essays.

6. If you are assessed by examination, who is the examining authority? _Polytechnique_

7. When do the examinations take place?

   March 81

8. Do you have to attend the college for a minimum number of weeks per year? If so, how many?

   6 months

9. How many assignments (essays, lab reports, etc.) have to be submitted during the year? When do they have to be submitted?

10. How many seminars (large discussion groups) and tutorials (small discussion groups) must you prepare talks for? When do these talks have to be given?

11. Which lectures are compulsory? When do they occur? Where are they held? Who are the lecturers?

12. Does the examination include an oral test of some kind?

13. Are you given any tests during the year? If so, when?

14. What is the name of your tutor and which is his room?

Equipment for Study

All students should get certain basic items of equipment. Tick each one off when you have got it and enter the details of the recommended books.

Folders: ring files (one for each subject) ☑

Pads of loose leaf paper ☑

Pens ☐ Pencils ☑ Rubber ☑ Ink

Past examination papers for each subject ☐

A dictionary ☑ A page-a-day diary (see page 24) ☐

RECOMMENDED TEXTS

AUTHOR	TITLE	PUBLISHER

2. Planning Study

When to Study

Now you have found out what has to be done, make a rough plan for the academic year putting in the deadlines for all your assignments.

	Assignments for the year
November	3rd : deadline for 1st essay 15th : seminar paper
December	12th : tutorial paper 18th : deadline for 2nd essay
January	14th : deadline for 3rd essay 22nd : Finish first draft of project
February	28th : seminar paper
March	5th : tutorial paper
April	17th : start revision 26th : ~~start revision~~ project deadline
May	2nd : tutorial paper ~~15th : project deadline~~
June	3rd : ~~finish revision~~ exams start ~~15th : exams start~~

When you have worked out all these details, make a chart on a large piece of paper and put it on your bedroom or study wall. The programme may have to be altered later on, so be prepared for this.

Make a similar timetable for your working week.

1. Write in the routine things which we all have to do – eat, go to the laundry, visit the shops, etc. We tend to underestimate the time these take, so think carefully.

2. Write in the lectures, seminars and tutorials you will attend.

3. Write in your social arrangments: for example, playing football on Saturday afternoons.

4. Then write in the study periods and say what you will be doing in each case.

   Arrange them as follows:

   (a) put in reading sessions before lectures so you can read up a subject in advance. A follow-up session after the lecture is useful as well.

   (b) allow one hour each day for reading over the day's notes to make sure you can understand them.

   (c) put in two hours a week for revision.

   (d) no single study session should be less than one hour or longer than three hours.

   (e) allow a five minute break after each one hour session and a longer break between longer sessions.

   (f) leave one day free and also Friday and/or Saturday evening. Don't study when friends are likely to be free.

   (g) refer to your year (or term) programme and make sure that all your tasks are covered. Some subjects may require more time than others.

   (h) keep two hours in reserve for emergencies.

5. The items under numbers 2 and 4 should make up a total of around 40 hours.

A typical timetable might look like this:

Time	Sunday	Monday	Tuesday	Wednesday	Thursday	Friday	Saturday
9		prepare seminar	general reading	shops	read for lecture (lab.)	reading for sociology essay (lib)	prepare for seminar (home)
10		→ (home)	→ (library)	→	lecture Rm. 15	→	→
11		lecture Rm 12	lecture Rm 22		general revision		(home)
12	lunch	check sources for essay (lib)	read for lecture			reading for essay → (library)	lunch
1		lunch	lecture room 12	lunch	lunch	lunch	laundry
2		reading for economics essay	general reading	reading for sociology essay (library)	tennis match ←	reading for essay → (library)	← cinema
3		break	break	break	←	break	←
4		reading for economics	general reading	general reading		lecture Rm 15	
5		essay library	→ (home)	→ (home)	→	general revision	→
6	plan week	dinner	dinner	dinner	dinner	dinner	dinner
7	dinner	write notes (home)	write notes (home)	revise notes (home)	revise notes (home)	write notes (home)	out! ←
8							

Now work out your week's work in this way. You may like to do this every Sunday for the following week. Some students also like to finish each day by making a note of the next day's tasks.

Sunday	Monday	Tuesday	Wednesday	Thursday	Friday	Saturday

Where to Study

You must also decide where you are going to study.

IN A LIBRARY

Some study, such as research for an essay or your project, will need to be done in the library. Other tasks, such as reading course books or revising lecture notes, you may prefer to do at home.

When you make out your study programme for the week, write in the places where you will be working. When you are thinking about this, keep the following points in mind:

1. Not all places are suitable. Do not attempt to work in a coffee house, a bar or the students' common room.

2. Choose a place which you can use for every session so that you will come to associate the place with study and be in the right frame of mind for work when you get there.

3. Be consistent. Once you have found a good place, use it regularly.

The library is a good place to study. Find out the following information about the college library.

1. What times of the year does it close?

2. What days of the week does it close?

3. What times of day does it normally open and close?

4. How many study places are there?

5. Can these be reserved?

The ideal place to study should have:

1. Enough light, so that you do not strain your eyes and get headaches.

2. The right temperature, which is about 18°C (63°F). If it is warmer, you will want to relax! If it is colder, it will distract you.

3. Adequate ventilation, otherwise the air will get stale and you may want to go to sleep.

4. A large desk or table.

5. An upright chair which is not too comfortable.

6. As little noise as possible. Some noises, especially people talking, are disturbing. Do not try to study while the radio is switched on.

7. There should be nothing to distract your attention. Your eyes should be focused upon the book or your notes.

8. Books for reference.

9. Freedom from interruption, for example, people asking asking questions or wanting to make conversation.

10. The sight of others working. Many people find this better than isolation.

Check whether the place you have chosen has all these.

Some students have to do all their studying in libraries because their home is not suitable. However, libraries tend to become overcrowded. It is an advantage to have a room of your own where you can study. To convert a room into a study, remember the following points:

1. If you can choose which room to study in, choose one which is not near the living-room, kitchen, or the front door.

2. If you can, use the room for study only. If you live in a bed-sitting-room and have to use it for other purposes such as sleeping or eating, it is sometimes difficult to study there. If the room has a bed, you may be tempted to study lying down. This is rarely successful! It is also more difficult to make sure domestic chores do not encroach on your study time.

3. Check the list on the previous page. Is the lighting adequate? Is there enough ventilation? Is the temperature right? Is there likely to be much noise or interruption?

4. Get some basic furniture. You should have a large table or desk, a desk lamp and a small bookcase for reference books. It is also useful to have some sort of filing system for your folders.

5. Put a large notice board on one of the walls, if you can. Pin on it:

   the regulations
   the syllabuses
   the list of lectures
   the year's programme.

6. If you are studying at the Open University, and do not live near a Study Centre, you may also want to buy a radio and perhaps buy or rent a television set as well.

7. Think carefully about the arrangement of the furniture. For example, place the desk near the window to take advantage of the daylight.

8. Those who live with their families have a special problem, as not all the members of the family may understand that there are several hours during each day in which you should not be interrupted. You must explain how important your study is.

9. Tell your friends which evenings you will be studying so that they do not visit your home and disturb you.

Record of Progress

A page-a-day diary was on your shopping list on page 15. You should use this to keep a record of your progress. Each evening write a brief description of the work you have covered during the day. If you have accomplished very little, it will remind you to work harder the next day. If you have covered quite a lot of work, the description will be good for your morale. Perhaps you have overestimated the amount of study you could complete in one day? If so, the diary will help you to alter your study time-table. Writing the description will also involve a quick revision of the day's work and this will help you to remember what you have learnt.

The description might look like this.

Thursday 8 February

9-10.30   Started feasibility study on equipment required for small generator

11-12.30   Neustatter lecture in Rm.15

1.30-3   Read ~~Page~~ Baldwin 100-150

3.30-5.30   Continued work for report on locations suitable for beacons near London airport

7-8.30   Prepared for tomorrow's tutorial

You should also keep a record of the marks you get for each assignment. Design a series of forms like the one below which could be pinned on your board:

SUBJECT : LITERATURE 1650 – 1800		
Date	Assignment	Mark
12/11/75	Essay on Richardson's novels	B+
15/1/76	Essay on Restoration Comedy – Congreve	B
3/3/76	Essay on imagery in Milton's 'Paradise Lost'	B+
7/4/76	Project on first three books of Gulliver's Travels	B
15/5/76	Talk on Pamela	A –

3. Libraries and Using Books

Libraries

To get the best use from your college library, find out the following information:

1. Where are the catalogues?

2. What catalogues are there?

3. Is there a subject catalogue or index?

4. Where in the library are the books on your subject kept?

5. Where is the reference section?

6. How many books can you borrow at any one time?

7. How long is the period of loan?

8. Do you have to pay fines on overdue books? What is the rate?

9. Where are the bound periodicals and journals kept?

10. Where are the current issues of periodicals kept?

11. Can you borrow periodicals?

12. Which periodicals does the library take on your subjects?

13. What reference books are there on your subjects?

14. Are the books on your reading lists in the library?

15. What is the procedure for borrowing books from other libraries (inter-library loans)?

16. Are there facilities for making photo copies?

There are three main systems of library classification. The Library of Congress Classification System uses capital letters followed by numbers. In this system history and topography are classified in the following way:

D   General History
DA Great Britain
     20–690 England
     700–745 Wales
     750–800 Scotland
     900–995 Ireland
DB Austria-Hungary
DC France
DD Germany

The Universal Decimal Classification (UDC) System uses numbers and introduces a decimal point for subdivisions for a subject. In this system, history is classified as follows:

930 History in general
940 History of Europe
941 Britain
     941.1 Scotland
     941.5 Ireland
943 Germany

The third system, the Dewey Decimal Classification System, is similar to UDC and also uses a decimal point.

Find out the classification numbers used in your library for the subjects you are studying:

Using Books

No single publication will provide you with all the information you need. There are many different kinds of publications – reference books, novels, periodicals, textbooks, newspapers, etc. – and there will be a large number of each on your subjects. How do you decide which to read? And then how do you read them all in the short time you have? If the student is not careful, he can spend so much time reading that he has no time left for the other things he needs to do. For this reason, you need to learn three skills when using printed material: first the ability to *evaluate*, to check quickly whether or not a publication is relevant and likely to be useful; second, the technique of *skimming*, of being able to find information in a book quickly; and third, the ability to *read quickly* and digest individual chapters or whole books.

EVALUATION

To find out quickly whether or not a publication is relevant and likely to be useful, check:

1. The preface and any other introductory material, e.g. the foreword. This will tell you the purpose and scope of the book and what type of student it is written for.

2. The author. Is he a recognized authority on this subject? What is his bias? Remember each writer has his own views.

3. The date of publication. The information may not be up to date. Perhaps there is a more recent edition of the book available.

4. Whether or not your lecturer has mentioned the book. Was the mention favourable? If it has not been mentioned at all, this may mean it is not highly regarded.

5. The footnotes and the bibliography. No mention of sources

and inadequate references may be a sign of unsound scholarship.

SKIMMING

To find information or ideas in a book quickly, look at:

   (a) the table of contents. This will list the chapter headings and may also include subheadings.
   (b) the index
   (c) subheadings in the text
   (d) chapter summaries if there are any
   (e) first and last paragraphs (or sections) of chapters, first and last sentences of paragraphs.

In four minutes find out the following information about this book:

1. Are footnotes mentioned in the table of contents?

2. Is there an index?

3. On what page does the subheading 'Checking Notes' appear?

4. On what pages are essay introductions discussed?

5. Does it describe how a bibliography should be set out?

6. Are there chapter summaries?

7. What is the first paragraph in Chapter 7 about?

8. Does the book mention tutorials?

9. On what page is interviewing mentioned?

READING QUICKLY

If as a result of evaluating a book and checking the index, etc., you believe it to be useful and want to use part or all of it for notes, read it quickly because there will be many other useful books you will need to use. In order to improve your reading speed, remember the following points:

1. Set yourself a time limit. As you read, look at the clock occasionally to check your progress. To keep up your speed, you must not linger over parts of the book or look back over pages you have already read. Try to increase your speed by allowing yourself slightly less time for each new book.

2. Train your eyes to see more. When we look at a page, our eyes tend to see only two or three words at a time as they move along each line of print. With practice, you can learn to read more effectively. Do this by moving your eyes down the *centre* of the page. Another movement which will help your eyes to see more is a zigzag down the page.

3. Remember what you are reading the book for. Concentrate on the main ideas.

4. Increase your reading vocabulary by looking up words you do not understand.

5. Some people read slowly because they have got into the habit of looking back at each sentence they have read. This is called 'regression'. The way to correct this habit is to set yourself a time limit so that you force yourself to keep moving forward.

6. Another bad habit is saying the words to yourself as you read as this tends to slow down your reading speed. As with regression, the only answer is 'active' reading where you force yourself to read a given amount in a set time.

7. The best way to increase your reading speed is to practise, each time cutting down the amount of time you allow yourself. Keep a record of your speeds on a form like the one opposite.

READING SPEED

Test no.	Date	What read	Time Taken	Number of pages	w.p.m.

Test your reading speed by finding the answers to the following
questions from this passage on the art of architecture (time limit
5 minutes):

1. For what is harmony a synonym?
2. The architect begins by assembling the basic elements of
   plan and . . . .
3. What is proportion in architecture?
4. To what do principles of design in architecture give rise?
5. In the light of what must each work of art be judged?

The Art of Architecture*

The art of the architect is to build aesthetically. Over and above the
objective requirements (to produce a sound and efficient structure which
is an expression of the needs of its users), he must endeavour to satisfy
the aesthetic sense by introducing abstract qualities of design. This
he does by using his sensibility to make a selection from the range of
elements available to him and combine them in a way that best
expresses his ideas and feelings about his theme. There is invariably a
choice between alternatives – arrangements, forms, materials – and it is
here that the architect is free to exercise his art.

All artists, whatever their media, express their intellectual and
emotional responses to their subject by shaping their material into an
image of some kind. They take the raw material of their experience,
select from it, and organize these separate elements until they have
imposed upon them an expressive 'order' or 'harmony'. In this sense
every genuine work of art is an original creation. Though historically,
in techniques and materials for example, there is progress, aesthetically
there is no such concept – only different kinds of achievement. This
we must always remember and be careful therefore always to judge
each attempt in the light of its own intention.

Works of art are not made to comply with any pre-conceived 'rules
of design', but if what are unequivocally acknowledged to be such

---

*Reproduced from *Architecture in England* by T. W. West with the
permission of the publishers, Teach Yourself Books Ltd.

by the consensus of informed opinion are scrutinized, they are seen to possess certain abstract qualities which may then be characterized as 'principles of design'. These in architecture give rise to specifically 'architectural values'.

As we have seen, harmony is nearly a synonym for design, and the elements of any composition are ordered by imposing a 'pattern' upon them. To be aesthetically satisfying this pattern must be endowed with 'unity', i.e. it must contain a dominant theme or centre of interest (focus or climax) and all parts must be related to the whole.

The architect does not consider the aesthetic problem as merely a question of applying ornament to a finished scheme, but begins at once by arranging his basic elements of plan and mass (not only in size, but in colour, tone, texture, strength and vigour of design) into a balanced composition, since 'balance' is a part of order. It need not be a symmetrical composition about an axial line, but should be free of 'duality' and have a well placed centre of gravity somewhere in the central area. In addition to its dominant focus the composition will probably have secondary climaxes, and accentuations or emphases.

It has been observed how the artist creates a pattern out of the material of his composition. Pattern implies the repetition of shapes, forms, lines, or combinations of these, which may be called 'rhythm'. In architecture rhythm occurs in three-dimensional forms such as the exterior grouping of blocks, roofs, domes, towers and chimneys, in the projections and recessions of the elevations, and in the interior spaces. It also occurs in the alternation of solids and voids and in two-dimensional surface patterning (of a fenestration system, for example). Whenever we recognize rhythm to which we instinctively respond, it gives us pleasure – always providing it is not monotonous.

Monotony is one of the principal faults which can occur in design. It is avoided by introducing into the general harmony a certain variety and relief through the quality of 'contrast', both in the major dispositions and in the details. The major forms, however, should be decisive, and despite contrasting elements there should be no hesitation about them. Thus a building should be either predominantly horizontal or vertical in its tendency and not hover indefinitely and irritatingly between the two.

In design, the relations between a part and the whole, or part and part, are called 'proportion'. Certain relationships or ratios are aesthetically satisfying for reasons which are not fully understood. Others, on the contrary, are distinctly uncomfortable. Attempts were made by the Ancients and by Renaissance theorists to find a mathematical basis for good proportion, but it does not seem to be susceptible to a purely logical approach. What is apparent is that decision of form is required in large masses, for a shape which is obviously neither a square nor a rectangle is disturbing to the spectator. On the other hand this kind of definition must be handled carefully in details, since it can create more centres of interest than are deliberately aimed at for the purpose of accentuation.

Further exercises in rapid reading can be found in Owen Webster's *Read Well and Remember* (Pan Books, 1965), Tony Buzan's *Speed Reading* (Sphere Books, 1971) and Manya and Eric De Leew's *Read Better, Read Faster* (Penguin Books, 1965).

4. Notes

Why Take Notes?

Many students attend lectures and read books without taking notes so we shall begin this chapter by listing the reasons why you should take notes.

1. Trying to take notes from a lecture or a book forces you to pay attention to it and to try to understand it. If you do not take notes, you may not concentrate.

2. Taking notes helps you to understand the book or lecture; even if you threw the notes away afterwards, you would probably remember quite a lot of what you had been reading or listening to.

3. You should not, of course, throw the notes away because your notes will provide material for your essays, seminar papers, etc., and will help you to revise for tests and examinations.

Materials

If you bought all the items on your shopping list (page 15), you should have several loose-leaf files (one for each subject), an assortment of pens (several colours) and a large quantity of file paper. The advantage of using ring files and loose-leaf paper is that the notes can be rearranged and stencilled handouts easily added. Leave the ring files in a safe place, and take a pad of blank paper into college each day. In this way you will be less likely to lose your notes or have them stolen.

Notes from Books

Your notes will come from two main sources – books (and other published material) and lectures. When taking notes from books, keep the following in mind:

1. Check that the book is relevant and generally considered useful (see page 28).

2. Start by making a note of the title of the book and the author. If it is in the college library, you should also note the classification number in case you want to return to the book later.

3. Use skimming techniques to find out which parts of the book are most useful (see page 29).

4. Read the chapter or section in full before you start taking notes. Only by doing this can you see how the ideas are organized and be able to reproduce this organization in your notes. Reading through first will also enable you to see which are the major points and which the minor. *You should note only the major ideas*; most students take too many notes.

5. On the second reading, make notes. Always try to use your own words. Make the notes as brief as possible.

6. Write down the part of the book from which you have taken the notes.

Some students prefer to underline, and make notes in, their course textbooks rather than take notes from them. Underlining in this way is useful but it must not be a substitute for taking notes. It is only by taking notes and forcing yourself to rephrase the ideas of the writer that you will really learn them.

Notes from Lectures

If you attend lectures, make the best use of them.

1. Read up about the subject in advance. This way you will understand more of the lecture and more easily how it relates to the rest of the course.

2. Sit near the front of the room so you can hear what the lecturer says.

3. Note the subject of the lecture, the lecturer's name and the date of the lecture.

4. Do not try to tape lectures. This is just postponing the task of note-making.

5. The lecturer will probably be working from notes which he has organized into sections. Listen carefully for words and phrases that indicate the organization of the lecture so that you can organize your notes in the same way.

6. Try to rephrase the lecturer's words.

7. Listen for the key points. Do not try to take everything down.

8. Ask questions if you do not understand.

Remember the lecturer is often the person who sets the examinations. His lectures may give some idea of what the exam will contain and how questions should be answered.

Notes from Television and Radio Programmes

Most of what has been said about lectures applies to television and radio programmes. As you cannot ask questions, concentration is very important. Sometimes programmes are repeated but you should always try to take notes on the first broadcast in case the subject is difficult and you need to listen to the programme a second time.

Note Layout

What sort of notes should you take? This will depend on what you want to use them for. If you are carrying out research for a project, you should use a card system which is flexible (see page 78). On the other hand, if you are taking notes for general use in essays, talks and for revision, the continuous notes taken on loose-leaf paper are suitable. While you are taking notes remember the following points about layout:

1. Leave plenty of space. In the example on page 44, a third of the page has been left blank. The reason for this is to allow room for further notes to expand upon the original notes or to make them clearer. Other ways of leaving space are writing on only one side of the paper or allowing a large gap between each line of the notes.

2. Number each point and use headings. It is much easier to use notes later if they are arranged in a pattern.

3. Use different coloured inks for the same reason. You could use one colour for headings and another for notes or write important points in different colours.

4. Use diagrams, charts, graphs, drawings and other visual means as often as possible. Pictures are more easily remembered than words.

5. Use abbreviations to save time but keep to standard abbreviations; do not use several different abbreviations for the same purpose.

Another way of taking notes is described by Tony Buzan in his book *Use Your Head* (BBC Publications, 1974). With this method, the main idea of a lecture or chapter in the book is placed in the centre of the page. The related ideas and facts are written around this and linked to the main idea by lines which show their relationship to it and to each other. The more important the idea, the nearer it is placed to the centre of the page. In these notes only single words and, occasionally, phrases are used. The result is a diagram or pattern. The advantages claimed for this method are as follows:

1. Because only key words and phrases are used, the notes are much quicker to write.

2. For the same reason, they are much quicker to read.

3. The notes are much briefer than conventional notes so there is a saving in space and paper. It should be possible to get all the ideas of a chapter on one page.

4. There is space available to add new ideas. Also the new ideas can be integrated into the existing notes and not just tacked on to the end or at the side somewhere.

5. The notes resemble a picture or diagram and are much easier to remember than words on a series of lines.

6. Most important, the notes reflect in their arrangement the relationship between the ideas in the book or lecture. Provided the key words and phrases have been chosen carefully, it it should be easy by a process of association to 'hook' all the ideas out of the brain.

This way of setting out notes is illustrated on page 45 Read the passage on industrial psychology which begins on page 40 and compare the notes on page 45 with the conventional notes on page 44. Which set of notes more accurately summarize the ideas in the extract? Which set do you prefer?

When starting to take notes, you might try using two pages at the same time – one for conventional notes, the other for Buzan's method.

People in Authority and their Subordinates*

The writer of Ecclesiasticus says that 'as the judge of the people is himself, so are his officers: and what manner of man the ruler of a city is, such are they that dwell therein'.

A modern psychologist says that 'the personalities of the leaders of a nation probably play a more effective part than any other factor in the peaceful working of the nation' (McDougall, 1920). If these statements be true of the heads of cities and nations, they are just as true of industrial organizations. The problem of the person in authority forces itself upon an investigator – sometimes as a disconcerting interference to the main investigation – but in the nature of things proof is difficult to obtain. It is not possible, for example, to grade a number of people in authority according to their efficiency and to have a psychological enquiry as to their intelligence, temperament, and character. What has been learned has usually had to be by observation or by interview.

It is self-evident that a person in authority who was too ignorant or too unintelligent for the post would either ruin the business or become a mere figure-head. But granted the intellectual and technical equipment, is there any evidence to demonstrate that the temperamental make-up of the head matters?

The most impressive standard would naturally be output, but in many occupations is is extremely difficult to measure efficiency or to have any objective criterion of success.

(1) In the experiment with noiseless typewriters it was pointed out that the effect of one of the heads of a group was to increase the average output of each of her group within a short time of her taking charge, and that the effect of another was to decrease it. The difference between the two was largely temperamental, one being extremely vital, emotionally well-balanced, while the other enjoyed ill-health. In reply to this one frequently hears, 'Well, we all know that'. The only answer is, 'If so, why don't we act on the knowledge more frequently?'

Another example, this time from a factory. The manager prided

---

*Reproduced from *An Introduction to Industrial Psychology* by May Smith (5th edition, Cassell, 1952).

himself on increasing the output by his mere presence. He was temperamentally childish, so on entering a room he usually shouted, grumbled – in short, threw his weight about. The consequence was a temporarily feverish activity which subsided on his departure. The object of an investigation into the effect of hours of labour was frustrated because the effect of the work was cross-cut by the manager's irregular appearances. On his departure, when the workers felt humorously inclined, a dramatic representation of his behaviour was given; they did not dislike him but rather despised him.

In another organization the head of the department was young, well educated, and inclined to be superior. In a detached, condescending way he treated his staff as automata. He was ambitious and anxious to get on, but his lack of imagination was patent in his lack of interest in his staff, and his treatment of them as a means to his ends, and a rather troublesome one at that. There was never any concerted effort made by the department to please him, whereas there was to save his charge hand from a row with him. In general his orders were ostensibly obeyed, because the staff were frightened of his sarcastic tongue; but had he only known it, he was silently obstructed in many ways.

Literal obedience can be two-edged. A man who demands it may find it used against himself, when subordinates, knowing he has made a mistake, may deliberately carry out his order.

(2) It often happens that work cannot be measured quantitatively, but in some occupations, where circumstances permit of finding other work elsewhere, the labour wastage is a good measure of management. There are many reasons for a high labour wastage, i.e. when employees only remain a short time, but among them is the kind of person at the top.

Two factories situated in the same town under the same general management, recruiting the same kind of labour, and doing the same kind of work, had a labour wastage in one year of 15 per cent and 55 per cent respectively. The labour manager had gone into the various environmental possibilities without finding any material difference, nor did the hours vary. The only discoverable difference was that the latter was in the charge of a man who bossed and bullied instead of leading, and the other was controlled by someone who knew how to rule.

(3) Where, however, there is contractual security, or the work is so highly specialized that other employment is unobtainable, it is found that absence because of sickness or other reasons varies according to differences in the temperamental make-up of the head. It is not suggested that this is the only, or even the chief, cause of a high sickness rate – the causes are many and difficult to disentangle – but it is one, and that not a negligible one.

The writer was at one time in daily contact with two groups of clerical workers over a period of several months. During a mild influenza epidemic on a certain Friday afternoon over 80 per cent of the workers in one room were absent, while in the other very few. The latter was in the charge of a well-balanced woman, while the other room was under a psycho-neurotic generally described as a nagger. Of the latter a typist who seemed ill and somewhat distraught said, when asked if she were ill, 'No, just 'er', pointing with her thumb.

The conclusion must not be drawn that the people were malingering. Of direct malingering there is little – probably most of us are not honest enough with ourselves to do that – but there is no hard-and-fast line between sickness and health, and a relatively slight condition may make all the difference between staying at home or going to work when the general circumstances make it easy to yield with honour.

In one factory the absenteeism for men was 6·7 per cent compared with 13·1 per cent in another comparable as far as work and general conditions were concerned, and 9·1 compared with 18·7 per cent for women. In this case, again the respective managers were the deciding factor.

(4) Sometimes it is the morale that suffers and a general attitude of grousing prevails.

The transport department of a large organization was afflicted with this disease, and when things had become so bad as to make it a general nuisance a Director tried to find the reason. It turned out that the departmental head insisted on having the vehicles put into the garage in a particular way, which the drivers considered made extra work. When an explanation was required he gave an excellent and unanswerable reason. When asked if he had explained to the men why he did so, he replied, 'No, why should I?' In that 'why should I?' lies the key to the difficulty. That attitude is the cause of endless trouble in industrial and even other relations. In this connection a letter appeared in *The Times* of Monday, October 19th, 1942, about a Tyneside shipyard strike. The writer complained that numbers of the workers were not consulted about an increase in their hours of work, and that they were expected to work under conditions imposed by agreements made without their knowledge or consent.

People in Authority & their Subordinates (May Smith
<u>Introduction to Industrial Psychology</u> Ch. 3)

Personalities of people in industry affect
those they are in charge of but it is
difficult to get reliable evidence of this

① The effect is not always obvious
    ⓐ Staff may obey when manager
       is there but not at other times
    ⓑ Obedience may be superficial

② Some evidence that personality
   of leader may be cause of high
   staff turnover

③ Also some evidence that leader
   may be cause of high rate of
   absence and sickness

④ The effect of a bad leader
   may be to produce bad morale
   and a lack of co-operation
   ("Why should I do this?" attitude)

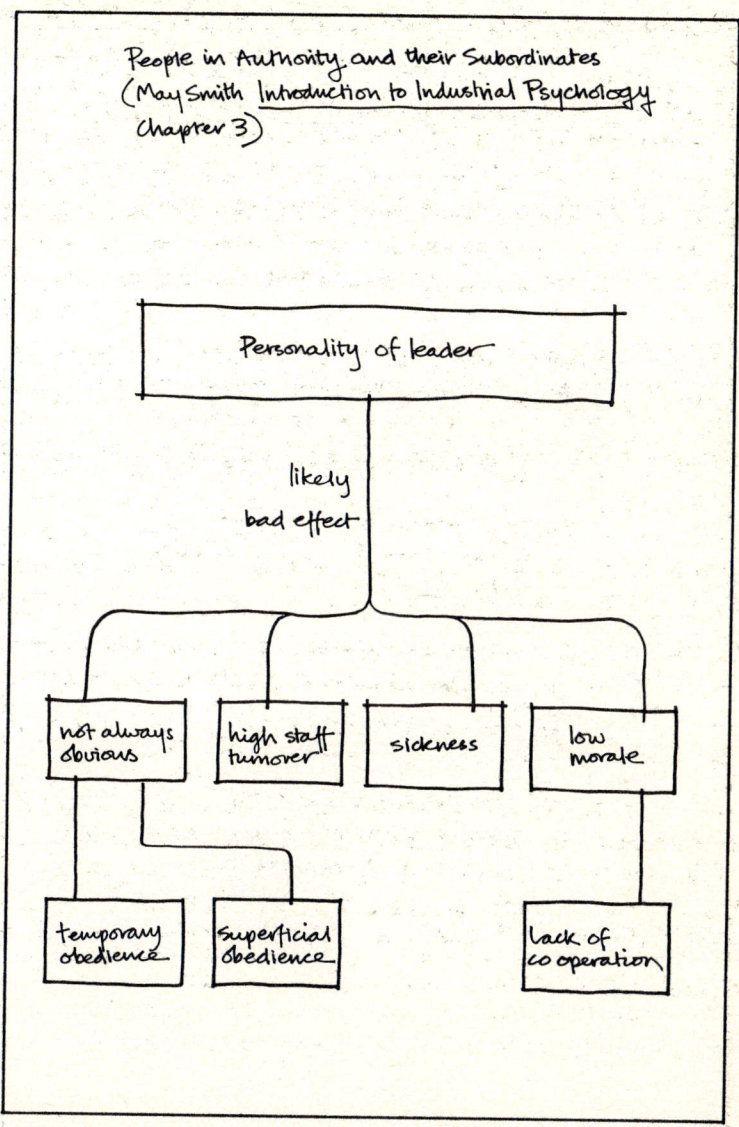

People in Authority and their Subordinates
(May Smith Introduction to Industrial Psychology
Chapter 3)

Personality of leader

likely
bad effect

not always obvious | high staff turnover | sickness | low morale

temporary obedience | superficial obedience | lack of co operation

Take notes from the following using the blank pages opposite and compare your notes with those on pages 44 and 45:

The Environmental Crisis*

When rockets from the Soviet Union and the United States travelled beyond the limits of the Earth and on beyond the moon to explore and report back on the state of our sister planets, Mars and Venus, they shattered what had been, for some, a fond illusion. The illusion was that perhaps we were not alone, that our neighbouring worlds may be inhabited by other beings, or inhabitable by man. But the photographs and instrument readings sent back to us from the planets most like Earth held no hope. One world was observed that is like the Earth might have been over three thousand million years ago – heated beyond the tolerance of life; and the other was not unlike the lifeless moon or perhaps like Earth may someday become if all life vanishes. We are alone in our corner of the universe, travellers on our beautiful, fragile, blue planet, shielded only by its atmosphere from lethal, life-destroying radiation from our own sun and from distant stars – radiation that would otherwise leave our lands as barren as the moon. Somewhere out among the stars there may be other planets like ours, but they are beyond our knowing at distances so great that generations of men would live and die before they could be reached by the fastest space-ship we can imagine.

Not very long ago and quite without the knowledge of most people, the human race was given power beyond any normal, rational comprehension – power that our ancestors, perhaps wisely, would have reserved only for the use of gods. The power came gradually – first fire, hundreds of thousands of years ago when men were few and could do little damage to the planet. But it was a force no other animal could use and man was to use it to change the lands that he inhabited. Next came the power of machines – simple at first and powered by hand, then growing more complex and finally to be fuelled by fire and water. Only recently man extended his sources of power when he learnt to tap the great reserves of ancient fuels – the coals, petroleum and natural gases, stored in the Earth over millions of years. Still

---

*Reproduced from *Planet in Peril? Man and The Biosphere Today* (Penguin, 1972) by R. F. Dasmann with the permission of U.N.E.S.C.O.

Rockets from USA and USSR

shattered illusions

more recently he discovered the secret of transmitting power over distances – through wires in the form of electricity and then without wires in radio waves. Using the materials of the Earth – its fuels, water, minerals – mankind could transform the surface of the Earth to a degree previously achieved only by the great forces of the planet itself – earthquakes and tidal waves, hurricanes and volcanoes. The human race could, and did, use the forces available to it to enrich life and enhance the existence of mankind. But the power that was achieved was not always used wisely. Man could, and did, also use these forces to make great areas of land and water barren – to create wastelands and to poison waters. Nevertheless, while men were still attempting to achieve wisdom in the use of the power already available, they were given the power that fires the sun. Held within the smallest components of matter, the forces that tie the atom together were beyond imagining – until the day when they were partially released by the first atomic explosion.

We are the custodians of the only planet friendly to life in the known universe. We have the power to make it lifeless. In our hands, today, rest the future of all known livings things. If we use our power wisely, life will continue to thrive on this blue planet and all of mankind may look forward to the future. But it is evident wherever we go on the globe that we are not moving fast enough towards the necessary wisdom. This is the basis of our environmental problems.

NOTES FROM *The Environmental Crisis*

Notes from Planet in Peril?
Man and the Biosphere Today Chapter 1

(c) learnt how to exploit
natural resources, ie coal
oil, etc

(d) transmit power
eg. radio waves

(4) This power not always used
wisely — pollution, the
atomic bomb

(5) We can make this planet
uninhabitable by humans.

(6) We must learn to use power
wisely

(7) Unwise use of power is the
cause of our environmental
problems

Notes from <u>Planet in Peril?</u>
   <u>Man and the Biosphere Today</u> Chapter 1

① Recent evidence from probes
   sent to neighbouring planets
   in solar system confirms that
   Earth is only planet in
   system with life

② May be life outside the
   system but this is too
   far away to reach

③ Human race has acquired
   through stages great power
   over its environment.
   In order

   ⓐ fire.
   ⓑ machines. Simple
      then complex. Powered
      by fire and water

Checking Notes

To make sure you have a good set of notes you should do the following each evening:

1. Remove the notes from the pad and put them in the subject file in the right place. The advantage of ring files is that notes can be arranged and rearranged in whatever way one wishes and that all the notes on one topic can be collected in one place.

2. Look over the day's notes for any careless omissions, un-readable words, points which are not clear. This is the time – while you still remember the book or lecture – to make sure that your notes are clear and that you will still be able to understand them in several months' time.

3. Write the sources and brief details of the day's notes in your diary.

5. Learning and Memory

Whether or not you pass your examinations will depend upon how well you learn each subject. This chapter tells you how to learn facts and ideas and also describes some techniques for memorizing information.

Learning

Many students think they can learn simply by attending lectures and reading a few books. In the last chapter, we saw that to do this without taking notes can be valueless to the student. Simply taking notes helps you to learn because you are forced to concentrate on the subject and to try to understand it. However, most learning results from the various ways in which you can work with your notes.

1. Re-read the notes soon after you have made them. The time when you are most likely to forget what the book or lecture was about is a few days after you have taken the notes. Re-reading the notes the same day should help you to remember them. On your study timetable you should have set aside some time at the end of each day for this purpose and this should be in addition to the time you have allowed for simply checking the notes.

2. If you were unable to organize your notes when you took them, read them through, putting in headings and numbering the points. Once you have given the notes a shape, they will be much easier to learn. Try doing this with the notes on page 44 and compare your structured notes with the example of page 56.

3. Add to your notes. Use the space at the side of the notes to

add additional facts and ideas from other sources (for example, a book on the same topic) or simply comments which make the original notes clearer.

4. Re-use your notes as often as possible. This can be done in several ways:

   (a) Reorganize them according to the topics in the syllabus and assemble all your notes on the same topic in one place. In doing this, you see how each topic fits into the overall scheme.

   (b) Re-write them, finding new words for those you have have already used. Try this with the notes opposite.

   (c) Summarize the notes in a series of points. Try this as well with the notes opposite. An example of how this might be done is given on the upper half of page 57.

   (d) Give an oral summary of the notes to another student.

   (e) Devise a series of questions to which the notes provide the answers. An example of such a list is given on the lower half of page 57.

   (f) Make the notes into a diagram, for example, large displays which can be pinned to the wall of your work room.

5. Follow these points throughout the year. If you do this, you will find you understand new ideas more easily. You will also find that you can remember large parts of the course without great effort. Do not simply put the notes aside until the exam. That way, you will find revision very difficult.

Notes from _Theses and Project Work_ Chapter 2

Arrive at a topic either because
tutor suggests it or because
choose it oneself

Students often choose wrong topic.
Common mistakes are choosing
too big a topic, one that is
too complex and requires too much
work, one that will take too much
time, one for which material is
inaccessible, one for which sources
of information do not exist, one
for which adequate techniques have
not been developed.

Must find out if material is available
and reduce the topic to suitable size.
Can narrow down by taking
one of standard approaches (eg. 'causes
of....) or by library research

When narrowing it down draw
up a sketch outline which will
form basis for discussion with tutor

Once topic and approach agreed,
can begin research. Many kinds of
research & kind used will depend on
topic

Notes from **Theses and Project Work** Chapter 2

The Topic — Arrive at a topic either because tutor suggests it or because choose it oneself

Pitfalls — Students often choose wrong topic. Common mistakes are choosing
(a) too big a topic, (b) one that is too complex and requires too much work, (c) one that will take too much time, (d) one for which material is inaccessible, (e) one for which sources of information do not exist, (f) one for which adequate techniques have not been developed.

Reducing the Topic — Must find out if material is available and reduce the topic to suitable size. Can narrow down by taking
(a) one of standard approaches (eg. 'causes of....) or (b) by library research

When narrowing it down draw up a sketch outline which will form basis for discussion with tutor

Kinds of Research — Once topic and approach agreed, can begin research. Many kinds of research & kind used will depend on topic

SUMMARY OF NOTES ON PAGE 55

Theses and Project Work Chapter 2

ⓐ How one arrives at a topic

ⓑ Difficulties in choosing a topic

ⓒ How to narrow a topic down

ⓓ The preliminary outline

ⓔ Discussions with tutor

ⓕ Starting research

QUESTIONS ON NOTES ON PAGE 55

Theses and Project Work Chapter 2

ⓐ How does one arrive at a topic?

ⓑ What are the difficulties in finding a suitable topic?

ⓒ How does one narrow a topic down?

ⓓ What is next stage?

ⓔ What is purpose of an outline?

ⓕ What determines nature of research?

Memory

In addition to following the general advice about learning in the previous section, there are certain techniques you can use to help you remember specific items of information:

1. If you want to remember a series of items (objects, facts, ideas), learn the first item on the list, then picture in your mind a story (the more absurd the better!) into which each item is introduced in turn. For example, in 1968 the seven largest manufacturing industries in Great Britain were, in descending order of importance:

   engineering
   food
   vehicles
   chemicals
   paper
   textiles
   metal

   To remember this, you might invent a story as follows:

   'I travelled back home on a train (engineering) on which I had a meal (food). When I arrived at the station, I went to fetch my car (vehicle) only to find it had no petrol (chemicals) in it. On the way home, I decided to stop for a newspaper (paper). As I got out of the car, I tore my jacket (textiles) on the door (metal) of the car.'

   The disadvantage of this method is that one can only recall any single item by going through the whole story in one's mind. The next method gets around this problem.

2. The second method of remembering a series of items, involves first learning a standard list of objects each of which *rhymes* with a number. A typical list would be:

one   : bun
two   : shoe
three : tree
four   : door
five   : knife
six   : fix
seven : heaven

You then remember your series of items by linking each in your mind with the appropriate rhyming word on the standard list:

one : bun : engineering
Imagine a train (engine) full of currant buns!

two : shoe : food
Imagine eating food (drinking champagne?) out of a shoe.

3. Most mnemonics (aids to memory) are sentences in which the first letter of each word is also the first letter of each item in in the list you want to remember. The following mnemonic helps you remember the names of the planets in the Solar System in order of distance from the Sun:

Men Very Easily Make Jugs Serve Useful Nocturnal Purposes. (Mercury, Venus, Earth, Mars, Jupiter, Saturn, Uranus, Neptune, Pluto)

A mnemonic for remembering the biggest industries in Great Britain in 1968 might be: Every Full Vat Can Please This Man

Devise a mnemonic for remembering metric measures: kilometre, hectometre, dekametre, metre, decimetre, centimetre, millimetre.

4. Yet another method of remembering a series of items is to picture in your mind an empty space such as a room or yard. Then put in a particular part of this room each of the items you wish to remember. For example the first item on the left hand wall, the second in the top right hand corner and so on. When you need to remember the items, you 'look around' the room in your mind. Try to learn the seven largest industries in Great Britain in 1968 by placing each in a part of such a room.

5. Rhymes can be a useful method for remembering facts. Perhaps the best known rhyme is one for remembering the days in a month:

Thirty days has September
April, June and November
All the rest have thirty-one
Except February alone
Which has twenty-eight days clear
And twenty-nine in each leap year.

A rhyme for the biggest industries in Britain might be:

First engineering, next is food
Third vehicles, then chemistry brewed
Five is paper, six textiles
Metal is seven – the list's compiled.

Invent a rhyme for remembering the planets in the Solar System or metric measurements.

6. If you find it difficult to use these techniques, write the items you need to remember on a small piece of paper and carry it around in your pocket. Each time you look at the piece of paper, you will remember more items.

7. There are some useful mnemonics if you are learning a foreign language (see the *Dictionary of Mnemonics* published by Eyre Methuen in 1972). Other techniques useful for memorizing languages are:

   (a) learning prefixes and suffixes which give a reliable clue to the meaning of a word.

   (b) associating the foreign word with a similar English word, e.g. '*livre*' (book) is easily associated with 'library'.

   (c) remembering that languages form groups with a common origin, e.g. Romance languages and Latin.

8. Maps are best remembered by associating the outline with a basic shape, e.g. a geometric figure like a trapezium. Once you have reproduced the basic shape, it becomes easier to introduce progressively more detail. Practice in this technique will help.

For more information on memory techniques look at Tony Buzan's *Speed Memory* (Sphere Books, 1971) or Ian Hunter's *Memory* (Penguin Books, 1964).

6. Essays and Talks

Essays and talks are the two most common tasks which students have to complete on a course.

The Purpose of Essays

Students often regard essays as a nuisance and try to avoid doing them as they interfere with the normal study programme. There are several reasons why the serious student should submit the required number of essays during his course and do them as well as possible:

1. Essays give you practice in expressing your ideas.

2. They are an incentive to work. Many students would do little reading if they were not required to submit essays.

3. The preparation for the essay involves re-using of notes taken from books and lectures and forces you to understand and learn a topic.

4. The essay gives both your tutor and yourself the opportunity to see how well you are doing with a subject. If the essay is poor, the tutor can explain what is wrong with it.

5. Together with your notes, the essay can be used for revision before the exam.

6. You will have to write several essays in each exam and you need practice in essay-writing.

7. The marks awarded for your essays may decide whether or not you pass the course.

Preparing the Essay

When you are given an essay to write, look carefully at the instructions.

1. What does the question mean? Make sure that you understand what is required. Ask your tutor to explain the instructions if you are not sure what they mean. Find out the meaning of any specialist terms in the question.

2. Look carefully at the key words which indicate the sort of essay and treatment of the subject that is required. For example, does your tutor want your opinion or not? Does he want a general treatment of the subject or a detailed analysis? In particular, look at words and phrases such as the following:

    What is . . . ? Give a definition explaining what the item in question is and how it differs from other items of the same kind.

    What is the significance of . . . ? Definition followed by an outline of its uses, consequences, results, conclusions, implications.

    Describe . . . Give a detailed description.

    Discuss . . . Explain, then give the pros and cons, implications, ramifications.

    Outline . . . Give the main points, leaving out detail.

    Comment on . . . Assess, give pros and cons of.

    Compare/Contrast . . . Look for similarities and differences between.

    Criticize . . . Give your considered opinion of, and present the evidence.

    Evaluate . . . Give your opinion of the worth of, in the light of facts.

3. Most important, what do you think the tutor wants to see in the essay?

How much research you do before writing the essay will depend on whether or not:

(a) the subject is compulsory
(b) the topic is one of those on which you have chosen to concentrate for the exam.
(c) the marks given for the essay will count for the course.

When preparing for the essay:

1. Re-read the essay topic and then write out a list of questions to which the essay should provide the answers. Do you already know the answers to these questions? Where can the answers be found?

2. Look at your notes on this subject.

3. Check whether your tutor has given you the titles of any books that might help with the essay.

4. Find out whether there are any titles on the general reading lists which are concerned with this topic?

5. See if there are any references to books mentioned in your lecture notes.

When you have completed the reading, sift through your notes and decide what you will include in the essay. The usual length for essay assignments is 700–1200 words and your essay should fall within these limits unless you have been given any other instructions. An essay of this length will have from 8 to 13 paragraphs depending on the number of major points. Write a plan for the essay, arranging the ideas into paragraphs (see opposite).

EXAMPLE OF AN ESSAY PLAN

Question : 'Compare and Contrast the use of the concepts of anomie and alienation in modern sociology'

Intro. Anomie often subsumed under alienation but it is separate (quote Nisbet) Essay will use Seamens five-fold classification as basis for discussion

Paras 1 & 2 Seamen one: powerlessness (see pages 10-13 of notes on Seamen and page 4 m Marx)

Para 3 Seamen two: mention Mannheim (notes page 8) and Parsons (notes page 24)

Paras 4 & 5 Seamen three : This on normlessness and anomie (Durkheim notes page 17 Merton notes page 3)

Para 6 Isolation (Durkheim notes page 15)

Continued

Organizing the Essay

There are certain standard ways of arranging the ideas in an essay:

1. According to time (chronological arrangement). If you are describing a series of historical events, start with the earlier period and move forward in time. For example, when writing about the history of a particular industry, you could start with the beginnings of the industry and progress through to the present day. This arrangement might also be suitable for a description of the development of a work of art or a series of poems.

2. According to place. If you are describing a country or town or a building, each paragraph could deal with a different part of it. In an essay about the economic geography of Nigeria, for example, each paragraph could describe a different region.

3. According to arguments. If you are arguing a case, each paragraph could put forward one of the arguments. In an essay in favour of the European Economic Community, you could devote one paragraph each to its advantages – economic, political, social, cultural, etc.

4. Simple to complex. Begin the essay by giving the overall picture and then go into greater detail. This arrangement is helpful to the reader if the essay is about a mechanism or a sophisticated piece of equipment.

Writing the Essay

When you write the essay, bear in mind the following points:

1. Before you start, try to put into three or four sentences what the essay is about. This should be a brief answer to the question. Doing this will clarify your ideas about the subject and make sure the essay keeps to the point.

2. Set yourself a time limit. You will have only about three quarters of an hour in the exam so allow yourself no more than one hour.

3. The first paragraph of the essay should introduce the subject and can be one or several sentences long. The purpose of this paragraph is to indicate what will follow and what your approach to the subject will be. It may include a re-statement of the topic together with an explanation of any key terms in the question.

4. In the main part of the essay, make sure you keep to the subject and that everything you say answers part of the question. Be tentative, never dogmatic, but do not be vague – support all you say with examples or by giving relevant facts or by referring to, or quoting, accepted authorities.

5. Include appropriate illustrations: diagrams, charts, maps, etc.

6. It is not normally necessary to number the paragraphs in your essay.

7. The last paragraph should sum up the main points in the essay and may resemble the outline suggested in paragraph 1 above.

8. At the end of your essay list the publications (and people) you have consulted for it.

Sample Essay

Describe and assess the tax system as a means of redistributing income.

Answer

1 The reduction of inequality of income or wealth is a task that occupies the State in a variety of ways. Taxation can limit the growth of large fortunes and the income drawn from their investment; subsidized social services can raise the real income of the poor by reducing the cost of certain items or by providing services that could not otherwise be afforded.

2 The tax system can be used to take from the rich and give to the poor. By steeply progressive rates of income tax and surtax, the State can keep earnings after payment of tax within relatively narrow limits. Progression in the tax system is achieved, first, by a system of allowances for family and other responsibilities and secondly, by differential rates of tax which cause the higher income groups to pay proportionately more than those with lower income. In the higher income groups, income tax is reinforced by the surtax which is also highly progressive, but which does not apply to the first few £1,000 of income.

3 By imposing death duties the State can prevent the passing of large estates intact to private persons. The rates of duty are progressive, varying according in the size of the estate.

4 However there are limits to the usefulness of progressive income taxes and death duties as means of redistributing income.

5 In the first place, a high rate of tax affects people's inclination to work. When a taxpayer's income reaches the point at which any further increase will be taxed at a much higher rate than he is paying already, he may decide that the net amount he can expect (from overtime, or promotion, or an expansion of his business) will not compensate for the extra work required to earn it.

6 In like manner steeply progressive taxes may reduce both the ability and willingness to save and invest. Death duties may discourage the accumulation of wealth, since one of the incentives to save is the desire to pass on the results of one's efforts to one's children. Further, an increase in taxation might lead to a reduction in savings by people who are determined to maintain their present level of expenditure.

Notes on Sample Essay

LOOK AT THE SAMPLE ESSAY OPPOSITE AND NOTE THE WAY IT IS CONSTRUCTED:

The first paragraph introduces the essay. It makes it clear that the essay will be about the ways in which the government uses taxes to redistribute wealth. The second sentence mentions each of the ways briefly and we are in no doubt at the end of the paragraph that the essay will consider them one by one in more detail.

The second paragraph opens the main argument of the essay. It deals with the first of the ways of redistributing income mentioned in the introduction. Notice the use of 'first' and 'second' to make each of the points clear. Note also that the writer has wasted no words; all the points are relevant and the phrasing concise.

The third paragraph deals briefly with the second way in which taxation attempts to prevent the 'growth of large fortunes'. This point could have been included in the second paragraph but making it the subject of a separate paragraph gives it greater emphasis.

The fourth paragraph is a transitional paragraph, which changes the direction of the essay. Note the use of 'however' which makes it clear that we are moving on to a different point. The use of transitions – words, phrases, sentences, or paragraphs which emphasize that the essay is moving from one point to the next – is very important if the essay is to read well. This way your various points will come across clearly and with impact. This paragraph announces the fifth and sixth paragraphs.

The fifth paragraph follows through the first of the writer's arguments against the uses of taxes on income and wealth to redistribute income. Note the use of 'in the first place' to stress that the paragraph opens a new phase in the essay.

The sixth paragraph continues the argument of the previous

7 There is a second group of taxes, in addition to those levied on the incomes or wealth of persons and firms. These taxes (often called indirect taxes) are levied on specific goods or services.

8 It appears that indirect taxes are almost certain to be regressive, that is, the lower income groups will pay a bigger proportion of their incomes in indirect taxes than do the high income groups. Those commodities which are heavily taxed, such as tobacco and alcohol, are very widely consumed and have demands which are inelastic with respect to price. If, as seems likely, the lower income groups spend a greater proportion of their income than the higher income groups on these commodities, there is a redistribution of real income in favour of those who are better off.

9 Expenditure on the social services (for example, education and health services; retirement and widows' pensions; insurance against unemployment and sickness; family allowances and child welfare services) has a very significant influence on the distribution of income since a large part of the total is devoted to transfer payments. The entire cost of these services is not borne by the taxpayer. Part is met from contributions by those who benefit from the expenditure. For example, National Insurance contributions cover most of the current outlay on pensions, sickness and unemployment benefit. Nevertheless, the social services do undoubtedly raise the disposable incomes of the recipients. The redistribution effects depend upon whether the bulk of taxation is paid by the wealthier members of the community. Certainly this is true of direct taxation on incomes and wealth, but there is doubt as to whether it is true of indirect taxation.

10 Thus a reduction in inequality of incomes has been achieved by steeply progressive direct taxes, as a result of which it has become necessary to have a gross income of approximately £10,000 a year in order to have about £6,000 a year after payment of tax. The accumulation of large fortunes is difficult partly because the ability to save has been reduced and partly because a progressive scale of death duties has greatly reduced the size of inheritances. Inequality of income is still further reduced by the provision by the State of social services which, though available to all, are generally of most benefit to people in the lower income groups. However, the effect of indirect taxation (which accounts for over 40 per cent of total tax revenue) seems to be a redistribution of real income in favour of the better-off households.

Notes on Sample Essay (cont.)

paragraph. The use of 'in like manner' shows the relationship of
this paragraph to the previous one. Note also the use of 'further'
in the last sentence to provide continuity and emphasis.

The seventh paragraph is transitional, like the fourth paragraph,
and announces the next paragraph. Note that it reminds us about
what we have just read ('taxes . . . levied on incomes or wealth')
as well as telling us what is to come ('taxes . . . levied on . . .
goods and services').

The eighth paragraph deals, as expected, with taxes on goods and
services. It advances a major argument against indirect taxes,
namely that they hit the lower paid proportionately harder than
the wealthier members of the community.

The ninth paragraph is the last paragraph of the main part of the
essay. It follows up the point announced in the second half of
the second sentence in the introduction: the way in which
government spending on social services effectively redistributes
income in favour of the less wealthy. Note the use of an example
in the third sentence and the transitional 'nevertheless' at the
beginning of the fourth sentence. As this paragraph makes
one of the major points of the essay, it is appropriate
that it is relatively long and that it is placed at the end of
the main body of the essay.

The tenth paragraph forms the conclusion to the essay (note the
use of 'thus' to indicate this). It briefly mentions again each of
the points made in the main part of the essay: the effect of direct
taxes (para. 2), of death duties (para. 3), of spending on social
services (para. 9). By choosing to reiterate the point made in
para. 8 in the last sentence of the essay, the author gives
particular emphasis to what he considers to be the disadvantage
of indirect taxes. Note the use of the emphatic 'however'.

---

* (Essay opposite reproduced from *General Certificate of Education
Advanced level Model Answers: Economics*, with the permission of the
publishers, The Artemis Press Ltd.)

Talks

The talks you have to do will either be seminar papers (for large discussion groups) or introductions to tutorials (small discussion groups). Before you start your research, check the following points:

1. Are you sure that you have understood what you have to talk about?

2. What is the purpose of the talk? Is it meant to cover every aspect of the subject, to encourage questions and discussion, or to introduce the topic.

3. Is yours the only talk?

4. How long are you expected to speak for?

The research for the talk will be carried out in the same way as for an essay (see page 63). However, the technique of writing a talk will be different in the following ways:

1. The main purpose of an essay is to demonstrate to your tutor your knowledge of a subject. As you can see from point 2 above, this is not the main purpose of a talk.

2. The audience for an essay is your tutor who will know more about the subject than you. The main audience for a talk is your fellow students.

3. A talk should not be written out in full. Simply list the main points that you will be making together with their references to the books from which you will be quoting. The purpose of this list is to remind you what to say. The information should be laid out as in the example opposite so that you can find your place quickly.

4. You have the opportunity to use audio-visual aids: for example, a blackboard.

Notes for seminar paper on
Formal Communications in Industry

① Outline of formal structures and
    channels: basic problems
    ⓐ size of organisation
    ⓑ getting cooperation

② Media of communication:
    relative merits and deficiencies
    (quote Ivens page 140)

③ Downward communication:
    magazines (show examples)
    bulletins (quote People at Work
    page 16) annual reports (show
    examples)

④ Upward communication:
    attitude surveys, joint
    consultation, suggestion schemes

⑤ example: Fawley agreement
    (quote Ivens page 318)

⑥ conclusions: principles & strategy
    (training schemes)

Bring Ivens <u>Practice of Ind. Comm</u>.
      Chisholm <u>Communications Industry</u>
      HMSO <u>People at Work</u>

Many students are nervous when they have to give their talk.
If you have no previous experience of public speaking, it is
difficult to present your talk well. One idea is to try the talk on a
friend. But perhaps the best way to learn is from the mistakes of
others. Notice the way in which other students present their talks
and use the chart below to assess them.

PRESENTATION OF TALKS

1. Did the student place himself so that he was facing his
   audience?

2. Did he keep his gaze on the audience?

3. Did he distract your attention with any irritating
   mannerisms; for example, by waving his hand too often?

4. Was his voice loud enough?

5. Did he vary the tone and pitch of his voice and his speed of
   speaking?

6. Did he speak clearly? Could you hear everything he said?

7. Did he use facial expression and the occasional gesture to
   make clear the meaning of his talk?

8. Was there any unnecessary hesitation? Did he ever appear to
   forget what he was going to say?

9. Did he use any aids to illustrate his talk; for example, any
   relevant charts, maps, or diagrams?

10. Did the speaker hold your attention? What was the talk
    about? Did it achieve its purpose? For example, did it
    stimulate discussion?

7. Projects

Nowadays many college and university courses require project work. This project may be called a report, special study, extended or long essay, thesis or dissertation. Students usually spend up to one year on the project and the completed essay is awarded a mark which contributes to the result of the course. Project work involves:

(a) choosing a topic
(b) defining the topic
(c) research
(d) organizing the notes
(e) writing a rough draft
(f) submitting the draft to your tutor
(g) revision
(h) preparing the final version
(i) submission of the project to the examiner
(j) sometimes an oral examination.

A project can be difficult and time-consuming. Students should set themselves deadlines for each of the major stages mentioned above. If the college year starts in September/October and ends June/July, use the following deadlines:

End of October	:	define topic
End of January	:	finish research
End of February	:	finish rough draft
End of March	:	finish revision
End of April	:	submit to examiners

You should try to complete the project before the end of April so that you can spend all the time before the exams on revision.

Research for Your Project

Before the end of October, complete the form on page 77 since these details will be wanted by your tutor before he will approve your topic.

When you have got approval for your topic, begin your research. Project work can involve all the following techniques of research:

1. Telephone inquiries. Prepare your questions before phoning. Have paper and pen ready. Explain who you are. Be courteous Thank whoever you are phoning at the end of the inquiry.

2. Letter inquiries. Set out the letter correctly. State who you are. Phrase the questions clearly. Thank the recipient in advance for assistance. Keep a copy of your letter.

3. Informal interviews. Prepare your questions beforehand. Explain who you are. Be courteous. Do not attempt to tape-record without asking beforehand. Thank the interviewer at the end of the interview.

4. Visits. Phone or write in advance. Do not take photographs without permission. Do not question employees in firms without prior permission. Be careful not to cause damage.

5. Survey work. Try out your questionnaire beforehand with a small group. Then work out the sample group to receive the questionnaire. Contact *all* in the sample. Do not presume too much from results.

6. Laboratory work. Get all the equipment you need. Set it up carefully. Record the results of experiment in the normal way.

7. Library research. The librarian will help you find information but find out where the main bibliographies and subject indexes are so that you do not have to rely exclusively on library staff.

Fill in the following broad details of your project.*

1. Provisional title:

2. Broad aim of essay

3. Outline of contents

4. Sources of information to be tapped:

   (a) documents (books, reports, articles, etc. – to be broadly identified):

   (b) interviews with:

   (c) visits to (specialist libraries, research organizations, installations, etc.):

   (d) other (specify):

* For detailed advice on project work, students should read *Theses and Project Work* by C. J. Parsons (Allen and Unwin, 1973).

Taking Notes

It is possible that you will take several thousand notes during your research and so you will need a system which will enable you to organize information easily when you write the project. Most students use cards because they are easy to arrange and carry about, and because they stand up to constant use. The cards can be bought at most stationers and are available in three sizes.

The card system requires keeping two sets of cards, source cards and note cards (see opposite). Source cards are for recording the details of sources of information. Every time you find a new source, write down a full description of it. If it is a publication, take down the following, *in this order:*

    (a) the author
    (b) the title of the article (if you are consulting a journal or newspaper)
    (c) the title of the publication (book, journal, newspaper)
    (d) the edition if not the first edition
    (e) the publisher (for books)
    (f) the date of publication

If, on the other hand, you are interviewing a person, write down the following information on your source card *in this order:*

    (a) his name
    (b) his status, e.g. Professor of Biochemistry
    (c) the organization, e.g. London University
    (d) its address
    (e) the date of the interview

The other set, note cards, is used for the notes themselves. In addition to the note, you also write down the subject of the note, the author or name of the person whose ideas you are recording and, in the case of a publication, the page. *Put only one note on each card.*

SOURCE CARD

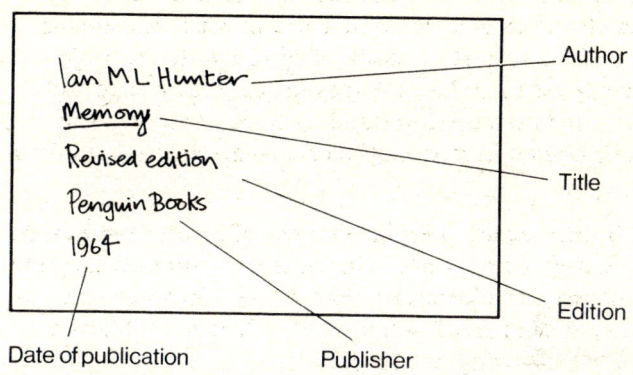

Author

Title

Edition

Date of publication

Publisher

NOTE CARD

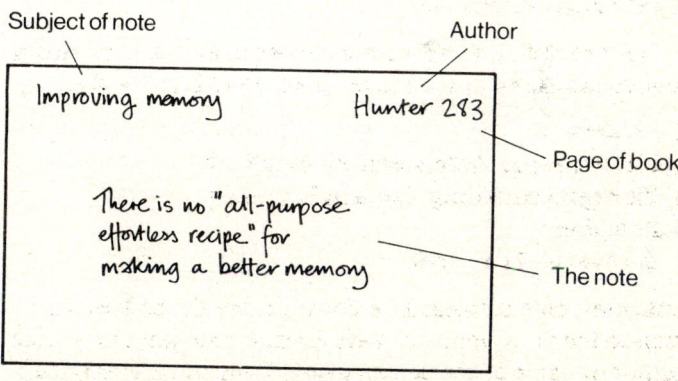

Subject of note

Author

Page of book

The note

Organizing Your Notes

When you have finished your research, collect your notes together and read through them.

Then put aside the notes you do not want to use. (There is often the temptation to try to include *all* the findings of one's research and you should be prepared to discard many of your notes.)

Arrange the remaining notes. The standard ways of arranging material (chronological, by space, by argument, overall picture then detail) were described on page 38. Since projects are much longer and their subject matter much more complex, it is sometimes difficult to keep to one of these standard arrangements and a combination of different arrangements may have to be used. For example, a discussion of events in two or more countries may have to involve a combination of chronological and space organizations. If you are faced with this kind of problem, remember the following:

1. Work out the organization in detail beforehand. Make a detailed plan.

2. Make the arrangement clear in the introduction.

3. Make full use of transitional devices, especially paragraphs which sum up what has gone before and announce the arrangement of what is to come.

4. Use cross-references, i.e. footnotes which refer the reader to other parts of the project which are relevant to the points under discussion (see the example on page 84).

5. Remind the reader in the conclusion of the organization you have used.

Presentation

The completed project should be written out neatly or typed. It must have:

1. A title page. In addition to the title of the project and your name, this should have the name of the college and the year. (see page 82.)

2. A table of contents. This should list the chapter headings together with the numbers of the pages on which each chapter starts. (See page 83.)

3. Footnotes. Whenever you quote from, or refer to, a particular source, the details should be given in a footnote. (See page 84.)

4. A list of sources. This should be placed at the end of the essay and contain details of all the sources consulted during your research. The items should be listed in alphabetical order of the author's name, and the details about each source should be given *in the same order* in which you recorded them on the source card.

Look again at the instructions on page 78 and at the example of a bibliography on page 85. Now work out what is wrong with the following references and add a correct reference for this book in (f).

   (a) Penguin Books: *Memory* by Ian Hunter.
   (b) *Theses and Project Work* by C. J. Parsons (Allen and Unwin).
   (c) C. D. Harbury *Descriptive Economics* 1972.
   (d) *Usage and Abusage*.
   (e) Fowler *The Kings English*.
   (f)

SAMPLE TITLE PAGE

LONDON COLLEGE OF EDUCATION

"English in Further Education"

by

David Shaw

1975

SAMPLE TABLE OF CONTENTS

CONTENTS

SAMPLE PAGE

However, GCE examinations are far from the only ones being offered in further education. English has for some years been an examinable part of many business studies and has more recently been formally introduced onto some engineering courses.

Most of the professional bodies in the business studies field include an English paper at Intermediate or Part One level. Among them are the Institute of Bankers, Transport, and Export, the Chartered Institute of Secretaries, and the London Chamber of Commerce. When one looks at the syllabuses and examination papers we find an interesting division between the traditional kind of paper where the emphasis is on the essay and precis, on the one hand, and what might be termed work-related questions on the other.[1]

Not all teachers are happy with a trend to work-related questions. Mr. P.N. Fletcher, Principal Lecturer at Avon Technical College, comments

> A lot that was useful in the more traditional
> paper has been jettisoned in favour of questions
> that do not necessarily give a reliable indication
> of ability.[2]

1. Pearce, John, "Essay and Work-related questions in ONC English" English in Education, Winter 1973, p.40.
2. Interviewed 10th March, 1974.

SAMPLE LIST OF SOURCES

LIST OF SOURCES

Interviews:

Dixon, M.J., Lecturer in Liberal Studies, Neasden College
    of Technology, London N6., interviewed 26th Feb. 1974.

Fletcher, P.N., Principal Lecturer in English, Avon Technical
    College, Bristol, interviewed 10th March 1974.

Thomas, T.W., Head of the Department of General Education,
    Eton College of Further Education, Bucks., interviewed
    6th March 1974.

Publications:

Clarke, David, "Examinations and the Aims of English",
    The Use of English, Autumn 1970

Clarke, Edmund P., "The Role of Language in General Studies",
    Liberal Education, July 1968.

Flower, Fred, Language in Education, Longman, 1966.

Pearce, John, "Essay and Work-related Questions in ONC English",
    English in Education, Winter 1973.

Smith, A.H. and Randolph Quirk, The Teaching of English: Studies
    in Communication, Secker and Warburg, 1959.

Whitehead, Frank, "Multiple Choice Comprehension Tests",
    The Use of English, Summer 1972.

8. The Examinations

Planning Revision

In your original timetable on page 16 you should have allowed four to six weeks before the examinations for revision. About two months before the examinations start, you should begin to plan your revision. Before you do this, check the following information:

1. The regulations. Your whole study programme should have been planned in the light of these but look at them again to make sure you have understood correctly which exams are compulsory and whether you have submitted all the assignments required.

2. The syllabuses. You should know these already but read them again to make sure you have understood them.

3. Past examination papers. Check again the length of the exam; the total number of questions; the number of questions you must complete; whether or not there are any compulsory sections or questions; whether or not there are any objective questions. Make sure you understand how the questions are to be answered.

4. Your own notes. Are they complete? If not, fill in the gaps now.

When you are satisfied that you have a complete set of notes and that you know exactly what will be required of you in the examination, then make out your revision timetable. Use the example on pages 88–89 and follow these instructions:

1. First write in each examination, indicating whether it is in the morning, afternoon or evening, its starting time and its length.

2. Write in the essential lectures which you want to attend during the revision period. The last lectures before an examination are often the most useful ones to attend.

3. Put in the revision sessions. Write in the topic (not the subject). Each session should be no longer than one hour. Allow for repeats of the same topic. Mix subjects so that in one morning you cover topics from three or four subjects.

4. During the revision period the total number of hours worked each week including lectures may be increased to 50 hours but should be no more if you are going to remain fresh for the examinations.

5. Do not put in any late night sessions.

6. Keep at least one full day and one afternoon free for socializing. Try to get away from the college and the tense atmosphere of this revision period.

7. Make a separate chart of the items on which you are concentrating for each examination. This will provide you with a total view of what you have to cover. Pin this chart on the wall and tick off the items as you revise them.

8. Allow at least four days completely free before the examinations.

REVISION TIMETABLE (partially completed)

Week ending 23rd April	Mon	prices; commodities; law of contract; H.P. Acts; international trade
	Tues	prices - commodities; law of contract; H.P Acts; international trade
	Wed	negotiable instruments; management theories; work study; bankruptcy
	Thurs	negotiable instruments; management theories; work study; bankruptcy
	Fri	prices-commodities; law of contract; H.P. Acts; international trade
	Sat	sales forecasting; markets; company law; public finance
	Sun	FREE
Week ending 2nd May	Mon	sales forecasting
	Tues	
	Wed	
	Thurs	
	Fri	
	Sat	
	Sun	FREE
Week ending 9th May	Mon	
	Tues	
	Wed	
	Thurs	
	Fri	
	Sat	
	Sun	FREE

	Mon.	
	Tues.	
	Wed.	
	Thurs.	
	Fri.	
	Sat.	
	Sun.	FREE
	Mon.	
	Tues.	
	Wed.	
Week ending 23rd May	Thurs.	
	Fri.	
	Sat.	
	Sun.	
	Mon.	FREE except for light revision
	Tues.	
	Wed.	
Week ending 30th May	Thurs.	
	Fri.	
	Sat.	
	Sun.	→

Preparing for Examinations

Now that you have planned your revision, remember these points about the actual revision:

1. It should be based exclusively on the notes whch you have built up from lectures, books, articles, etc., and on the essays, test papers and projects corrected and returned to you by your tutor.

2. Go over the learning and memory devices you have been using during the year. If you need to devise more mnemonics re-read Chapter 5.

3. Reorganize and rewrite your notes in the form of essay plans. These plans, only one on each sheet of paper, should contain in outline *all* the information required for a full answer (facts, references, quotations, maps in full). You should also do a separate plan for every question which might come up. Large record cards can be used instead of sheets of paper and these have the advantage of being more portable.

4. Read the plans over and over again. Test yourself continually even when you think you have remembered all the items.

5. Do timed answers, trying if possible to complete the questions inside the time limit you will have in the examination.

6. Do not isolate yourself but at the same time do not allow conversations with other students to make you anxious about your progress. If you have planned your revision thoroughly, you can be confident. Mix with students studying different subjects from yourself.

7. Do not use pep pills or other stimulants unless a doctor has prescribed these. You should be able to work 50 hours a week for two months and it is unwise to attempt more.

8. Do not work exclusively at home. Remember the advantages of library study mentioned on page 20.

9. Be firm with yourself over the four day rest period before the examination. During this time you can occasionally glance over essay plans but do not attempt more.

10. See your tutor immediately if you have any problems.

On the day before the examination, keep in mind these tasks:

1. Check and tick off:

   (a) the place of the examination (and number of the examination centre)
   (b) the starting time of the examination
   (c) your candidate number
   (d) your equipment (pens, pencil, ink, rubber, watch, any books, other items such as slide rule, geometrical equipment)

2. Go to bed early.

3. Set the alarm so that you have plenty of time to get washed and dressed, have some coffee with your normal breakfast and arrive early for the examination.

In the Examination

In the examination itself, follow this procedure:

1. Find out if a particular part of the room (or a particular seat) has been assigned to you. If not, and you can choose where you sit, place yourself where there is plenty of natural light and where you can see the clock clearly.

2. Make sure that your watch and the clock in the exam room tell the same time. Take your watch off and put it in front of you.

3. When you are given the exam paper, check that it is the correct one. (There may be two or more exams taking place in the same room.)

4. Read the instructions. How many questions have to be answered? Are any compulsory? Are there answer booklets to be completed? Are there any objective test questions? If so, where are the answers to be recorded? How much time have you got for each question?

5. Read through all the questions and tick those you think you can do.

6. Re-read the questions you have ticked. Check the phrasing, noting particularly the key words (mentioned in Chapter 6). These will indicate what the examiner is looking for.

7. Make notes for each question. Switch from one question to another, jotting down all the ideas that come to mind. Visualize the essay plans. Use the memory devices you learnt during the year.

8. Put your name, candidate number, course and any other information required on the exam answer sheet.

9. Break up the number of questions to be answered into time limits, e.g. first question by 9.55, second question by 10.40, etc. Start with what you think is the easiest question and,

using the notes, write your first essay. Remember the advice on essay writing given on page 63. Glance at your watch frequently to make sure you are keeping within the time limit. Write clearly and neatly. When you have finished the easiest question, go on to the next easiest and so on.

10. When you have finished all the questions check your script. Is your name on each piece of paper? Are all the answers numbered? Read over your answers for misspellings, omissions, miscalculations, etc. Join the answer sheets together. If there is an answer booklet, attach any additional sheets to it.

It is very important for you to finish the required number of questions; otherwise your paper will not be marked out of the maximum number of marks. If you miscalculate the time, so that you are left with, for example, two questions to do in 40 minutes, write two plans rather than one complete answer – one good essay may collect 14 or 15 marks out of 20 but each plan could get 8 or 9, that is 16 to 18 marks.

When you leave the examination room, it is not usually a good idea to discuss the paper with students as, for no good reason, you may get the impression you have not done well. Mix instead with people on other courses.

Take the rest of the day off. If you have other examinations over the next few days, try to keep your work down to light revision.

Conclusion

Studying well is not always easy because most of us are not naturally efficient. Effective study means developing efficient habits – planning ahead, thinking in advance about what, when and where you are going to study. It also means having the determination to keep to a plan since plans are of little use if you fail to keep to them.

Whether you are studying for personal satisfaction or because you have to, you will find essay work, tests, and examinations much easier if you develop systematic habits.

Being systematic means using books effectively, taking usable notes, revising frequently, continuous self-assessment – in short, following all the advice given to you in this book.

Study can be a pleasure or a burden. I hope that reading this book will enable you to gain satisfaction and success from your studies.

Student's Notes

Student's Notes